Hello,

Also Available in eBook and
XL Editions!

For Us

For You

A question before we begin:

Who are you?

If you are having trouble, just answer easily and naturally.

Soul

Mind

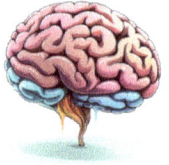

Body

Welcome All Humans!

Hello and welcome to
"A Hitchhiker's Guide to Humanity." Reading this page marks the beginning of a new daily journey that is intended to be exploratively experienced as a sideshow while you casually go through this life. Throughout each day for the next 4 weeks there are specifically selected activities conveniently scheduled around a 40-hour work-week for you to check out and check off! Each day's activities are broken down into open time-frames and minimum suggested durations because everyone's schedules, preferences, and styles of operation are different! So roughly by the sun in the sky or exactly at the same time each day, however suits you best, there are activities to complete every morning, afternoon, evening and night.

This guide is pocketbook size so you can have it with you throughout your day and easily flip it open on the go when it is time to check in! The main goal of this journey is to improve yourself in some way, each day. Sometimes just relaxing is the best way to improve yourself, so feel free to do so when you need. Take things one step at a time. Watch yourself live life. Learn to organize your time more efficiently, discover yourself, create new positive habits, advance old ones, and still have free time of your own! You can work on all of these fun things while simultaneously experiencing a spiritual side journey. Meet and observe your true self. Constantly acknowledge its separation from mind and body, thus unlocking a deeper understanding of life! With this understanding follows an unshakable internal peace, ultimately allowing you to be far less affected by daily stress.

Sounds amazing, right? It is!

If not... at least your place will be cleaner.

Daily Navigation

Let's take it step by step and look at how to navigate the journey ahead. First off, pick what you consider to be the Monday of your work-week as the first day to begin. On that first morning when you turn the page, you will see symbols...

Time of Day Indicator

Morning tasks are to be finished before you start the work day. Afternoon tasks are done during lunchtime.
Early evening and nighttime tasks are finished some time after work.

Daily Navigation

Afternoon

Under the time-of-day indicator, you will find symbols depicting the tasks ahead. For example, the task below is called a Mind Check. It is comprised of the Mind Logo paired with the Check Logo, creating the Mind Check Task. Fill or mark the check box however you desire after you complete the activity.

(Mind Logo)

(Check Logo)

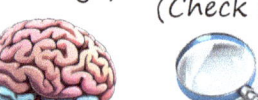

Check Box

Minimum Time Suggestion

Under the symbols are thought-provoking questions and statements, sometimes

Daily Navigation

related to the task at hand, sometimes not. Think about them, write about them, or ignore them, whatever works for you. After you have deliniated your task (in this example, Mind Check), flip to the back of your guide to find the corresponding Reference Page for the task. Look for the same symbols at the top of a page in the back to find more information on what to do during these activities.

(Try it now?) If you have extra time during a task and are busy, feel free to move on. If not, spend it thinking about ways to advance in that subject. Try to stay present for the minimum time even if you just close your eyes and breathe. It may take a little bit to get a pattern down, so just take it one step at a time.

Example of the calender day counter logo found on each day.

Hi, I'm Notey!

To Reader,

I'm here to tell you that each day ends with a notes page for you to freely use however you desire. Some ideas include: jotting down reflections on inner thoughts, answering questions that arise internally or that you are asked externally, taking notes, making workout routines, keeping track of progress, making to-do lists; there are so many options! The lines are faded in case anyone wants to use the space for charts or drawings!

From Notey

Packing List

Some things to have ready before we begin:

A Physical Book

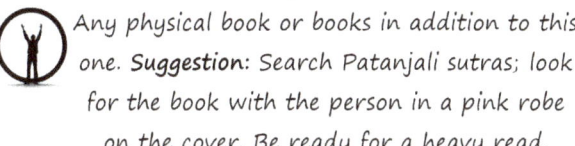

Any physical book or books in addition to this one. **Suggestion:** Search Patanjali sutras; look for the book with the person in a pink robe on the cover. Be ready for a heavy read.

At Least 1 Topic of Interest

Some topics to expand your knowledge on. It can be anything from knot-tying to not crying and can change or be revisited. What do you wanna learn about?

fill it, check it, x it, color it, who cares!

If you haven't already, and you want to flip ahead and see what to be ready for and when, go for it!

The Reference Pages in the back are key. Make sure to check them out. Find and read the "Always Remember" page with this symbol

at the top before you begin your daily journey. Carry and expand on this message throughout your travels. Take this time to prepare.

Flip this page

on your

work-week

Monday

morning!

Brick by brick, building a foundation we go! With each swing of an axe we are closer to a warm fire for the evening. Taking a step-by-step approach is sooo mainstream because it is extremely effective. If you really want to get something big accomplished or changed in your life, it helps to slow down and respect the intricacy of the process. Take things step by step and you will arrive at your goal.

Start!

Day 1

Time of Day Indicator

(Mind)

 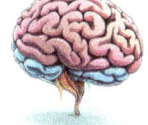  
2 min

Flip to the reference (Check)
pages when needed!

5 min

(Home)   (Check)

Quick home check: What needs to be
cleaned up before I start my day?

(Body)

Quick body check: What areas do I need to address?

 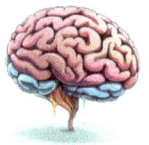  

Looking at this evening it sure looks like a lot, but it will be easy. If need be, the Mind Gain is there to give you time to learn and plan what you're going to do for the following Body Stretch.

 **Evening**

 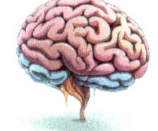  

Before dinner? After? You pick.

(Gain)

(Stretch)

 **Nighttime**

 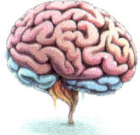 

(Daily Notes Page)

Morning

Day 2

 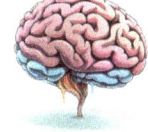  

What do I needa have with me or have done?

After a home check, there is no open food out. At the very least, the plates are in the sink soaking or cleared and in the dishwasher, if available. Any crumbs and/or spills are addressed.

Goal: Prevent Insects/Bad Smells

Afternoon

Pick up where you left off yesterday? New thoughts? Focus on your physical body.

 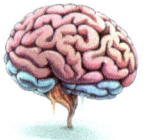  

Quick mind check: addressing our current life procedures and their status.

 Evening

Day2

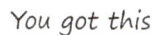 You got this!

 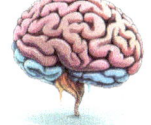   10 min

    10 min

(Move)

 Nighttime

   5 min

 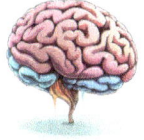   3 min

Reading books makes the brain "buff."

 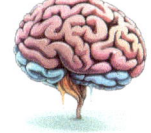  

Anything to pay, or monies to check up on?

Quick cleanup before starting your day, even if you are working from home.

Who do you want to be physically?

 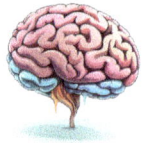  

Around lunchtime, check back in with
making your life run smoothly.
Anything to remember?

 **Evening**

 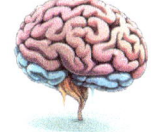   10 min

    10 min

 **Nighttime**

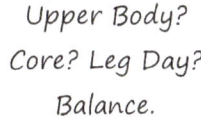 Upper Body? Core? Leg Day? Balance.

   5 min

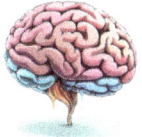   3 min

 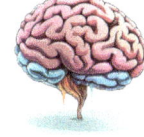  

Wow, what a week so far!

Liberation Lake?

Imagine: You wake up by a lake after a night of camping. If you could do anything, what would you do?

If you are having trouble forcing yourself to be healthier, try convincing yourself instead.

 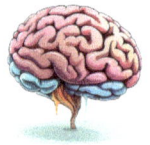  

Gain inspiration for becoming healthier by remembering your reasons for doing so in the first place. **Disinterest yourself in bad habits by instead becoming interested in how good you feel when you shed them.** This is where you will find actual satisfaction.

 **Evening**

 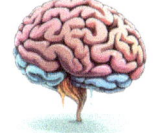  

Use this Mind Gain for body movement research of your interest.

 **Nighttime**

Body Move: what did you do earlier this week? Switch it up?

 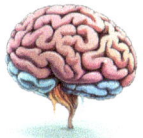  

 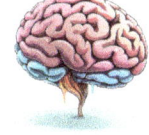 

You know this one.

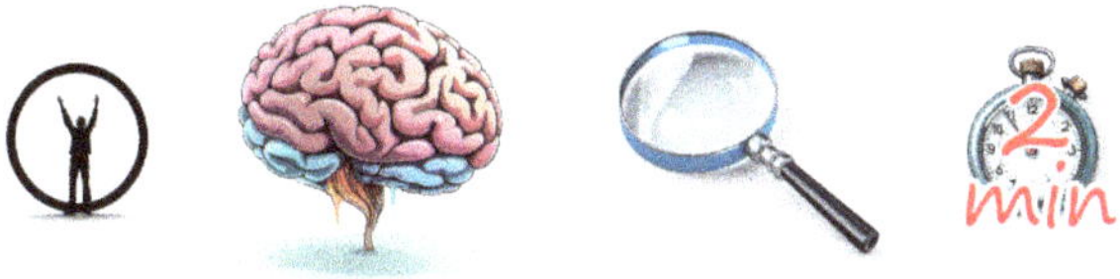

Friday!?

Have your healthy eating habits earned you a cheat day on the weekend?

 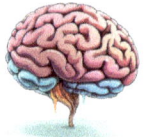  

What do you have to get done before your weekend starts?

 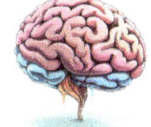  

 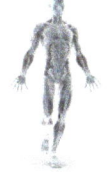  

Try something new? Advance in something you know and like?

Only words for tonight. Is it the start to your weekend? Whatever the circumstance, here is something to think about: **Make an effort to appreciate where and when you are, instead of what you are doing or not doing.**

Hey, it's Notey, seeing if you
are using the notes pages? If
I'm in your way, I'm sorry!
But I want to say Hi. So, Hi!

Day Off?

There is nothing for you to see here!

The next page is intended to be your
Saturday afternoon. It is more of a weekend
thoughts segment and will continue for each
of the 3 following Saturdays.
Relax Enjoy Peace

Your home is a shelter for your car and your body. Your car is your body's vehicle. Your body is your soul's vehicle and a shelter to your mind. Your mind runs the body as the engine runs the car.

Both are vital for operation and must be maintained. However, neither make the overall decisions. The driver of the car is making the decisions. This is your soul, your spirit, separate from all. It experiences the trials and tribulations of this world through your body to purify itself by making good decisions and helping others. Think of the world as a training ground for your soul. The more good you do, the better tools you have to use the next time around, your next life, your next chance. Each time you are faced with a choice, simple or complex, and you make the right decision, you move in the direction of purifying your soul. That is why the right decision is not often the easy one. You must challenge yourself to advance yourself. It is true with all things.

The point is to advance so far that you become liberated from human desires. You become enlightened and are no longer bothered by worldly dramas or emotions like anger and greed. You have successfully realized those are just temporary distractions that take away from true happiness.

Close your eyes...

Breathe

 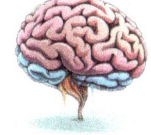  

Today's a good day to hang around the house doing chores.

Some laundry while simultaneously food prepping for the upcoming week? Organizing things after an adventure weekend? Random Sunday tasks, so for this reason, there is no suggested time.

Yoga was designed to help us connect within.

(tap)

Your first Soul Tap is later tonight. Look inside. Focus on trying to realize, appreciate, meet... you, your soul, the watcher. At the very least, just nose breathe and meditate. Breath is energy; breath is power.

By Sunday night the goal is to have the home clean...

 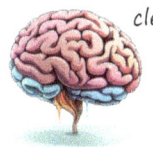  

...and clutter-free, ready for the start of a new week.

(Soul)　　Get within.

Start your morning with the thought that no matter what happens to you today, good

 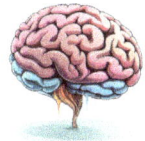  

or bad, it doesn't affect your internal being. Protect your internal contentment.

Clean home for the body, clean home for the mind, clean home for the soul, clean being within.

Afternoon

Bad food is a temporary pleasure with negative body results, a double loss.

 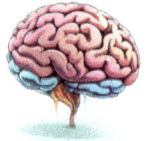  

If something brings you comfort but is also causing you guilt, then work towards rewarding yourself with what you want, just...less often.

 # Evening

Body stretch and gain 10 min each!

 # Nighttime

Lift weight for your body. Think & Read for your mind.

Look inside for your soul.

Did I discover anything about myself last night?
Or just close my eyes and breathe? Both are
good.

 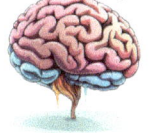  

Enjoy **when** you are, appreciate the briefness
in the grand scale of things...

Do I have a clean home?

Am I taking care of my soul's vehicle, my body?

 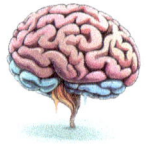  

In life you MUST follow your own path; otherwise, the destination you arrive at will not be your own!

 Evening

 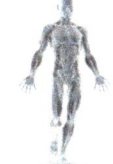   10 min

Move for your body.

    7 min

 Nighttime

Learn for your mind.

  5 min

    1 min

Be real in who is you to separate the soul.

If you can't truly listen and be honest with yourself, how can you expect to get anything done within?

 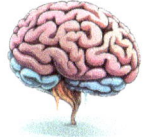  

Do you need to make a To-Do or To-Get list for anything?

If your house is usually clean, think of ways to improve your cleaning process or ways to better organize your things.

Afternoon

What does this body that I am currently in need for proper nutrients?

 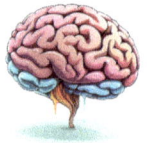  

What color fruits and veggies have I been skipping? Mix it up!

 **Evening**

   20 min

   7 min

 **Nighttime**

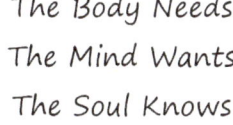

The Body Needs
The Mind Wants
The Soul Knows

  5 min

   1 min

Whatever the world throws at you today, remember it doesn't hurt the soul, just your mind.

 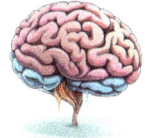 

-Checking in with life stuff-

Diet fuels the engine (your mind), that runs the car (your body), operated by the driver (your soul).

If you went hiking by a river, would you take 5 minutes to-pause music-Close Your Eyes, breathe in fresh air, and listen to nothing but nature?

 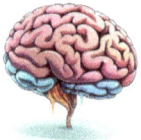  

Deep Relaxed Breath

 **Evening**

    10 min

   7 min

 **Nighttime**

Think about what thoughts, behind thoughts, are causing feelings.

  5 min

    1 min

Maintain a bird's-eye view of one's actions. Watch yourself.

 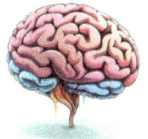  

When having trouble deciding something, go with your gut,

because even if you're wrong, you know that you trusted yourself.

What is the point to life?
Life with a point.

 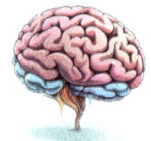  

If you're a good person, you only have to worry about defeating the bad in the world. Look to work with other good people, not against. More is gained that way. Always beware of con artists. Evil runs on greed and must worry about competing against other evil as well as good. If you do the right thing, it is better and easier for the long run.

Evening

Nighttime

Helping others actually helps you.

Jealousy from comparison with another person is foolish. The minute that you put yourself above one, you place yourself behind countless. Appreciate competition, but don't let it define you.

Throughout life's negative social games that have no real winners anyway, if you don't play, you can't lose.

As a human, you get better at life. As a soul, you get better at being. If you are worried about social praise or having the newest things, you are worried about advancing your human self in what you already know is a temporary life. Make the connection that your soul is the primary objective. It doesn't use physical possessions to advance itself. Help others and do the right thing, especially when it is difficult.

Advance your soul.

Just as car engines drive themselves with features like auto pilot, it is a worldly temptation to allow the mind to take over. It is easy to get lost in temporary satisfaction. This can happen to anyone, even those aware of their temporary hitchhike in this human body. Advancing the soul requires work and attention. A moment of awakening can take place over time or can be instant. A whole new view of the truth can be seen; a world that is a beautiful training ground for the soul, in which we are lucky to have a chance to experience, is realized. Of all forms of existence, in only the human form is it possible to reach the ultimate goal, a pure soul's enlightenment.

Some people are consumed by photos, the past. Enjoy your past, but stay moving forward. Enjoy your memories, but don't obsess.

Sunday funday! Take comfort in the relaxing nature of it.

 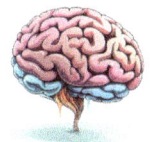  

Back to Earth, unless you already wanna move to a mountaintop and become a guru... there are life things to do. Check in.

You are battling your demons daily to become the best you, you can be. Like a warrior, use great attention to detail on **all aspects** of your being.

Afternoon

Boredom is your fault.
Boredom is a periodic lack of will to use imagination, in association with the lack of will to do something, or create something for your own enjoyment, gain, or the gain of others. Yet, you retain the desire to be entertained. If you take this to heart you should never be bored again. Do something, think about others, learn something, or simply enjoy not having anything to do.

 **Evening**

 Day14

   ?min

 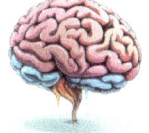   5 min

 **Nighttime**

eyescloseddeepbreath
breathedeepclosedeyes

  2 min

    3 min

New week, new experiences, new lessons.

 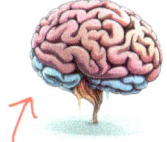  

How do you feel now compared to
the first time you saw this?

Everything turned off before you leave home?

Back to healthy eating routines.

 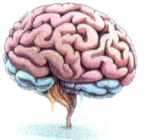  

Breathe, Relax, Smile

 **Evening**

   **30 min**

   **10 min**

 **Nighttime**

Ordinary externally, extraordinary internally.

  **7 min**

   **2 min**

Life is a gift, not a punishment. It is an opportunity. If it seems difficult,

 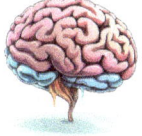 

maybe you have karma to work out from past lives.

Own it and focus on being better at humanity. For you, for us.

Afternoon

It's not fair to have unspoken
expectations of someone.

 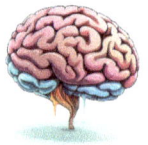  

The fault is not on them for failing to
meet your unclarified expectations; it's
on you for expecting them to.

 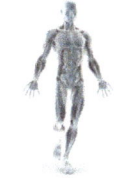  

Plant thoughts,
cultivate ideas.

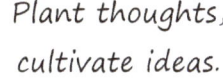

 **Morning**

    2 min

Watcher of Mind

Separate:
Soul, Mind, Body

 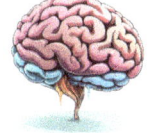   2 min

Mind life stuff.

    5 min

A clean place for your mind to move
your body through life as your soul
watches, learns, and gains.

Sometimes the admission of the lack of knowledge is a display of knowledge.

 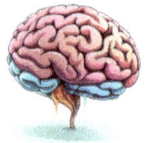  

It's easier to trust someone when they show you they will admit if they don't know something. Furthermore, pretending to know and giving false information can cause more harm than just admitting the truth.

 Evening

   30 min

   10 min

 Nighttime

Either you will have patience or you will have stress.

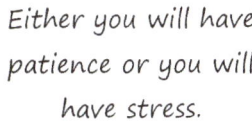   7 min

   2 min

Go in your own direction before you end

 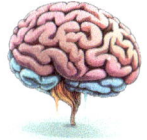  

up somewhere you don't wanna be, with

less of the only thing you need to fix it:

time.

If you were on a mountaintop after a good hike, would you be better able to picture a bird's-eye view of yourself, watching yourself?

 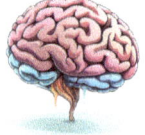  

 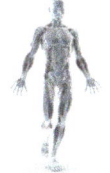  

15 min

10 min

 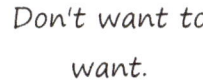

Don't want to want.

7 min

2 min

Morning — Day 19

It's   Do something nice   2 min

 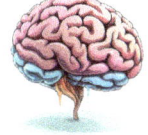 

finally   Smile   2 min

"Friday"   Be content with yourself   5 min

Any changes in you this week?

 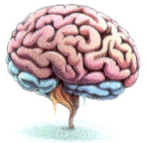  

1 really slow, really deep breath through the nose. Eyes shut.

 **Evening**

 **Day19**

 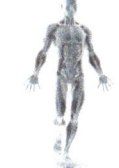   **1.5 min**

 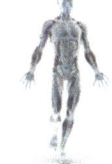   **1.5 min**

 **Nighttime**

Aim to be a knowledgable person, not an acknowledgable profile.

    **2 min**

If you can't be comfortable with yourself, then who can you really be comfortable with? You must learn yourself first; then, you can become the best you, you can be: in relationships, in business, in life.

The world IS what you think it is. If you think it's a great place, you are right. If you think it is a terrible place, you are right. It is all up to your perception. How you see the world becomes your reality. In the big picture the world keeps turning just the same. There are countless good things happening and countless bad, with no way of really knowing which is more widespread for certain. ***Happiness is your choice made within.*** If you can make the decision that you want to be happy, every day will be one filled with an unshaken internal joy. Focus on not letting common daily external events affect your internal contentment. Work on not letting even the biggest events affect your soul. Life is cyclical in nature.

Love Yourself, Love Others.
For You, For Us.

If happiness isn't enough, you will never be satisfied.

Hint:

Help Others
Help Yourself

If you are afraid to do something that you believe will make you better,

 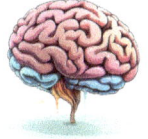  

then safely do it BECAUSE you are afraid to. The sense of gain is amazing.

Week Prep

Gain happiness from simplifying your life, not from buying material possessions. By taking this approach you might feel like you are missing something because you are not buying things, but in reality you are gaining freedom from attachment. Fill the need to gain with the sense of freedom.

Evening

Day21

? min

 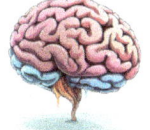  

7 min

Nighttime

How nice treats can be when enjoyed occasionally.

3 min

4 min

Morning

Day 22

Constantly watch your thoughts as they enter your mind.

 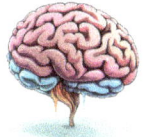  

What are you keeping track of?? Or are you totally locked in already, in all facets of life?

Deep clean every 6 months to a year. Pull everything out of everywhere, condense, donate, clean.

Should I learn more about cooking to make eating healthy more enjoyable?

 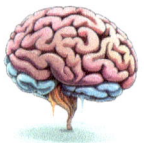  

The more things you want, the more you must do, the more you must stress.

 Evening

 Day 22

   1 hr

   10 min

 Nighttime

Choose happiness.

    10 min

   3 min

As you challenge your soul,

 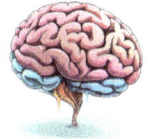 

challenge your mind,

challenge your body. Advance Yourself.

Bad days happen. When you are having an off day, the key is to first accept it.

 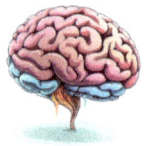  

They happen to everyone. Do your best to prevent it from getting worse. Maybe it will get better, maybe not. Go to bed early. Whatever happens, don't let it get worse by letting it affect your mind. Remember your soul, your true self, is unharmed.

 **Evening**

    30 min

   10 min

 **Nighttime**

Comfort can bring complacency.

  10 min

   3 min

Advance Some Way

Never spend time wishing away time.

 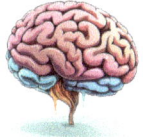  

Time is the only thing you will never get

back with the opportunity you have now.

It's tough to do things when you can't do things, because things are in the way!

 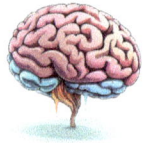  

...You can always find other things to do to be productive while you are delayed.

Don't get mad, get better!

 **Evening**

   1 hr

   10 min

 **Nighttime**

Do Good

Be Good

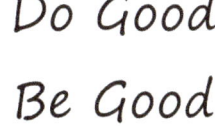   10 min

   3 min

Experience may be the best teacher;

 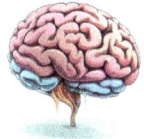  

in actuality it is **YOU**. How you gain from

your experience is the determining factor
in whether the lesson is learned or lost.

When is the last time you took a trip to the ocean, or any large body of water and just relaxed?

 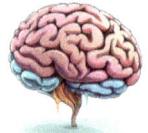 

 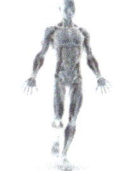  

30 min

10 min

Who do you want to become?

10 min

3 min

Teach Yourself

 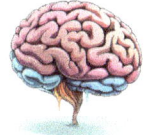 

Listen to Yourself

Learn

Never forget

 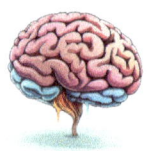  

True happiness is a choice, your choice. It can only be given to you by you, and taken from you by you.

 **Evening**

    **30 min**

    **30 min**

 **Nighttime**

Love your body.
Improve your body.

    **3 min**

Be the best you, you can be.

Have you felt that change inside when you read a really good quote that hits you in just the right way?
Take a second to think about it.
See if you can recreate that feeling inside right now...
The point to a good quote is to inspire change, but you are the one that makes the change. It is not because a bunch of catchy words are cleverly strung together, but instead because YOU pull out the courage to change within.

Picture your bad habit, bad mindset, or whatever you wish to overcome as a rock you must carry. One day you are able to finally free yourself of it and cast it in the water. It splashes and begins to settle to the bottom, causing ripples on the surface all the way down to the waterbed. Once you cast the rock in the water, the ripples that ensue can be compared to memories of indulging in these desires and can cause the want to indulge again. As long as the rock stays at the bottom, over time, similar to the ripples in the water, those temptations lessen and eventually dissipate. Maybe in this life or the next, who knows? The ultimate goal is to be able to enjoy the world without requiring any bonuses for your true happiness. Just being happy to be alive is the mindset.

Don't get stuck in a rut unless it is positive for you, then find tributaries. Branch out from positive enjoyment to expand yourself.

Morning

Who

 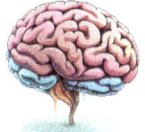 

Are

You?

Never feel like you don't deserve what you are as a being, good traits or bad. Work with your good ones, work on the bad ones. Turn a weakness into a strength. Utilize your skills to make the world a better place. This can help disprove irrational thoughts of underserving or inadequacy.

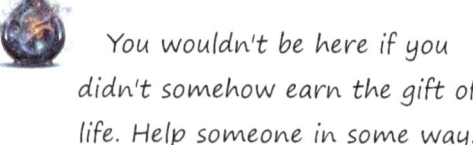

You wouldn't be here if you didn't somehow earn the gift of life. Help someone in some way.

 Evening

   ? min

 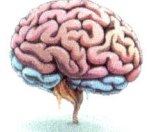   10 min

 Nighttime

Simple wants lead to extravagant gains.

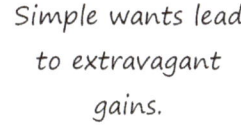   3 min

    5 min

Finish!

Final Celebration
Circle Check Box!
Did you do your
best?

Hopefully, you can walk with more
of a sense of liberation and
happiness.

Pages

Always Remember...

I retain my peace constantly because I believe my soul is separate from my mind and body. It is eternal. Nothing in the physical world can affect it.

My soul, known as "my true self" or "the seer" only learns from the experiences of pain, happiness, and emotion. Therefore, I should never be controlled by them.

I KNOW my peaceful state is not in overjoy or sadness, but instead always present with a joyful contentment for the blessing of life.

O

Soul Tap

Goal: Realize What You Are (Eyes Closed)

Realize

Who am I? My soul can't be classified by physical aspects or titles such as gender or occupation. I am an eternal spirit.

Look

What must I focus on to become who I need to, furthering my soul for the good of us all?

Act

How am I implementing lessons learned about myself to increase positivity in general throughout my current time on this earth?

You are an eternal being that, in this moment of opportunity, is a blessing of formed human energy. Do something good with it.   1

Soul Check

Goal: Separate + Watch Thoughts (Eyes Closed)

Target

Close your eyes. Pick a thought on your mind.
What thoughts behind this thought caused it?

Feel

How is this thought making me feel?
Why do I feel this way?

Learn

Is it positive or negative? Either way, I'm
separate from it. It is all formed by my mind,
while my soul watches and learns.

Remove the desire for desire.
Watch thoughts as they enter your mind.
They are only necessary lessons for the soul. 2

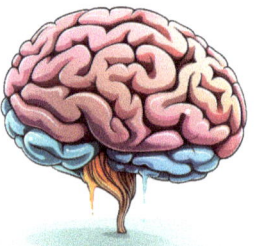

Mind Check

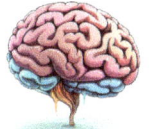

Goal: Smooth Life Operation

What do I need to have with me for what I need to get done?

Life Needs, Work Needs, Store Needs, Gas? Clothing? Return Texts? Calls?

Birthdays, Anniversaries, Holidays, Gifts, Returns, Preparations?

Bills, Reoccuring Charges, Registrations, Insurance, Certifications, Payments, Identifications?

W
h
a
t

A
m

I

F
o
r
g
e
t
t
i
n
g
?

3

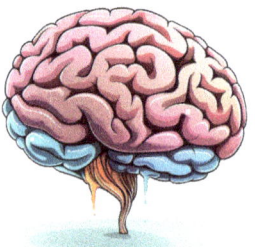

Mind Stretch

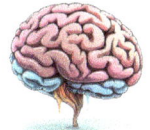

Goal: Read A Physical Book

During this activity, pick up an actual book. Reading a physical book is an excellent way to increase brain activity and is often overlooked. So whether you are a seasoned reader, or a NOT reader, your chosen reading times may vary. One thing for certain is the book you're reading right now doesn't count! Pick up something for entertainment, or education, or switch off between the two. Go wherever your mind takes you!

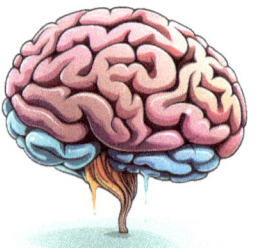

Mind Gain

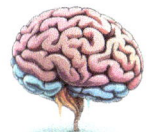 

Goal: Increase Knowledge On A Topic

Use books, computers, friends' knowledge, anything to learn about whatever you want! The focus could be directed towards finite things, like skills that are useful in daily life, or intangible subjects, like life's meaning. Research topics that interest you. If you have hobbies, learn more about them. Learn how to be better in them. If you don't have hobbies, learn more about yourself and look into what you would like to pick up. Learn about meditation, self-realization, and anything else that may be useful in accordance within this book.

Find desire, then aspire.

Body Check

Goal: Maintain Physical Body Health

Do I drink enough pure, unflavored water?

What can I eat to better balance my nutritional intake? Think food group variation. Some new things to cook?

Should I change up something about my physical workout routine to incorporate a muscle group or activity that I have been overlooking?

Any meds to take? Physical therapy stretches?

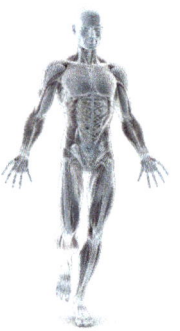

Body Stretch

Goal: Become More Flexible

During this activity you are to focus on flexibility. Incorporate movement or remain static and focus on your breath while stretching. Do stretches you know and love or learn about new styles in your Mind Gain sessions and try them out.

Yoga is an excellent way to work on flexibility, strength, discipline, and soul, all at once. There are many different types to try, so do some research and see what appeals to you most. A good start for a newbie is looking into restorative yin yoga, a lower-intensity class to ease your way in, gradually trying more styles if you are interested.

7

Body Gain

Goal: Gain Strength

This task addresses strength. Strength is extremely important for so many reasons other than just lookin' good. Having strong muscles protects your organs and body structure, preserving its performance in the long run. It is a natural suit of armor. Don't waste it, upgrade it. Research new schools of thought and plan during Mind Gain sessions.

Areas to Address

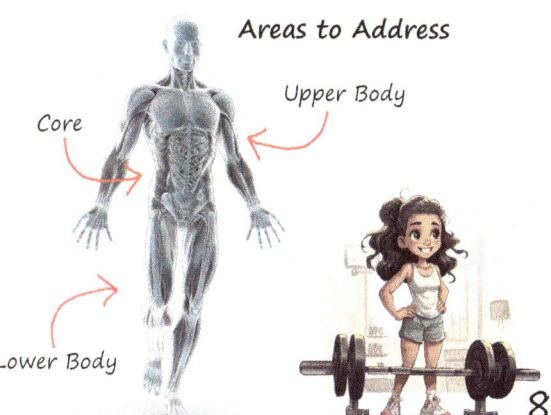

Core

Upper Body

Lower Body

Body Move

Goal: Increase Cardiovascular Capabilities
With flexibility and strength being addressed, there is one more basic avenue to pay attention to: the cardiovascular system. SO many options here! Depending on where you're growing athletically, adjust the intensity of each activity. Research walking, running, hiking, biking, all things cardio!
Get out and move!

Activities

Swim

Cardio Tools

Run/Walk

Home Check

Goal: Maintain a Clean Household

Make the bed or just tidy it.

Clear any food mess + dishes.

Spray and wipe down counters.

Clear clutter.

Vacuum somewhere.

Laundry on Wednesday and/or Sunday...?
Other than the obvious health advantages,
having a clean and organized life operation
center often leads to having a more organized
and clean mind, ultimately leading to the same
results for life overall.

10

Copyright Page

I hope this helped in some way.

Written and Created by
Casey Graves
A special thank you to
D&M + C&M

A Hitchhiker's Guide to Humanity

ISBN: 979-8-9905177-0-7
Contact the Publisher
Immaculation LLC
930 S 4th St, Ste 209 #4139
Las Vegas, NV 89101
immaculationllc@yahoo.com

Also Available in eBook and XL Editions!

Please rate and review your experience.

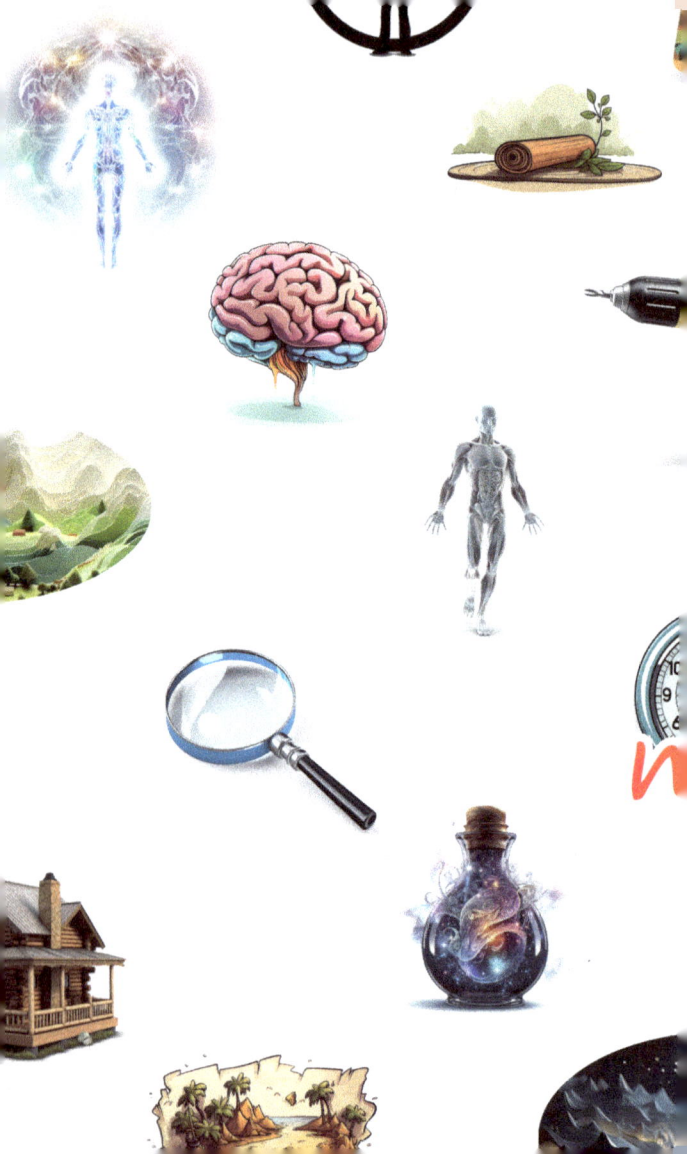

www.ingramcontent.com/pod-product-compliance
Lightning Source LLC
Chambersburg PA
CBHW051203120626
46547CB00012B/1187